Maestro Heights Museum
Our Remarkable People

The Strenuous Life of Scott Joplin
Ragtime Composer

Copyright © 2020 Gail Masinda

All rights reserved. No part of this book may be reproduced or transmitted in any form or by any means, electronic or mechanical, including photocopying, recording, or by any information storage and retrieval system without the written permission of the author, except where permitted by law.

ISBN 978-1-7346937-0-6

Storyboards created using StoryboardThat.com

Published by Maestro Heights
www.gailmasinda.com

Maestro Heights Museum
Our Remarkable People

The Strenuous Life of
Scott Joplin
Ragtime Composer
ca. 1867-1917

Gail Masinda
Maestro Heights, Galesburg, Illinois

Contents

Welcome to Maestro Heights...iv

The Story of Scott Joplin...1

Maple Leaf Rag FAQ..8

The Story of the Crush Collision..14

Politics, Ragtime and Opera..26

Treemonisha and Heartbreak..29

Awards, Memorials and Legacy...34

Resources and Credits..47

Hi! Welcome to **Maestro Heights**! I'm Gail, your teacher and guide. There are many places to explore and things to learn here in our town. Today we are going to visit the museum to check out the exhibit about the remarkable composer, Scott Joplin. Let's go inside!

This is a multimedia exhibit! Point your smartphone to this QR code. It will take you to a special collection of music, videos and extra information on our museum website.

No smartphone? No worries! Go to:

https://gailmasinda.com/maestro-heights/museum/scott-joplin/

The passcode is: **RAGTIME**

(case sensitive passcode!)

Throughout this book you will find these yellow tickets. They show you there is more to explore in the online exhibit.

JOPLIN Online Exhibit

"Wrong is never right,
You will agree with me;
Wrong is never right,
And it will never be."

~Scott Joplin, *Treemonisha*

The Story of Scott Joplin

Scott Joplin! Even while people loved his music and called him the "King of Ragtime," Mr. Joplin was concerned his music wouldn't be remembered. Sadly, he was almost right. It was about 50 years AFTER he died that people came to recognize his innovative and creative genius. Here is his story.

Father Jiles Joplin was born into slavery in North Carolina. He was a musician who played the violin. Mother Florence Givens Joplin was freeborn in Kentucky. She was a musician, too. She played the banjo and sang.

The Joplin family, Jiles, Florence and their son Monroe, were living near Linden, Texas, when Baby Scott was born around 1867. The family moved to the Texas side of Texarkana, a city split by Arkansas and Texas state lines. Before Scott started school, the family moved to the Arkansas side of town.

Jiles and Florence had four more children after Scott: Robert, Osie, William, and Myrtle.

JOPLIN Online Exhibit

This is the Orr School in Texarkana. Scott attended school here in the 1870s.

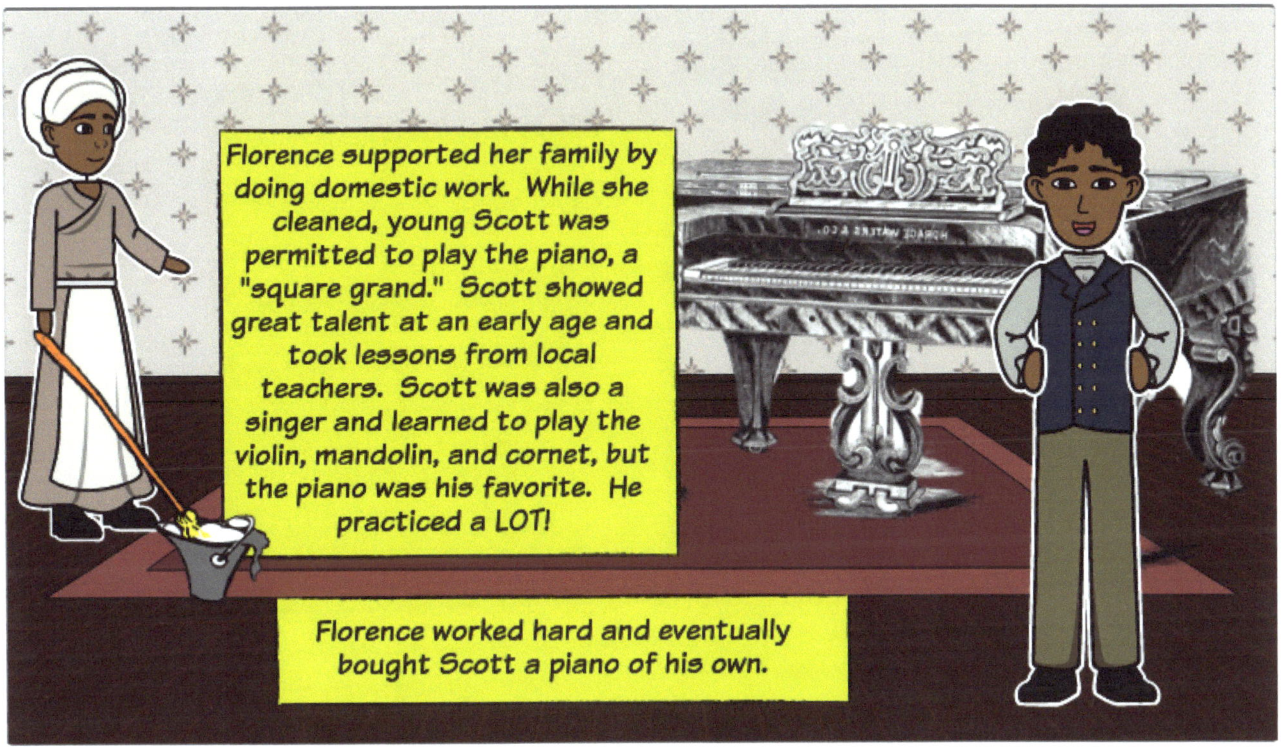

Florence supported her family by doing domestic work. While she cleaned, young Scott was permitted to play the piano, a "square grand." Scott showed great talent at an early age and took lessons from local teachers. Scott was also a singer and learned to play the violin, mandolin, and cornet, but the piano was his favorite. He practiced a LOT!

Florence worked hard and eventually bought Scott a piano of his own.

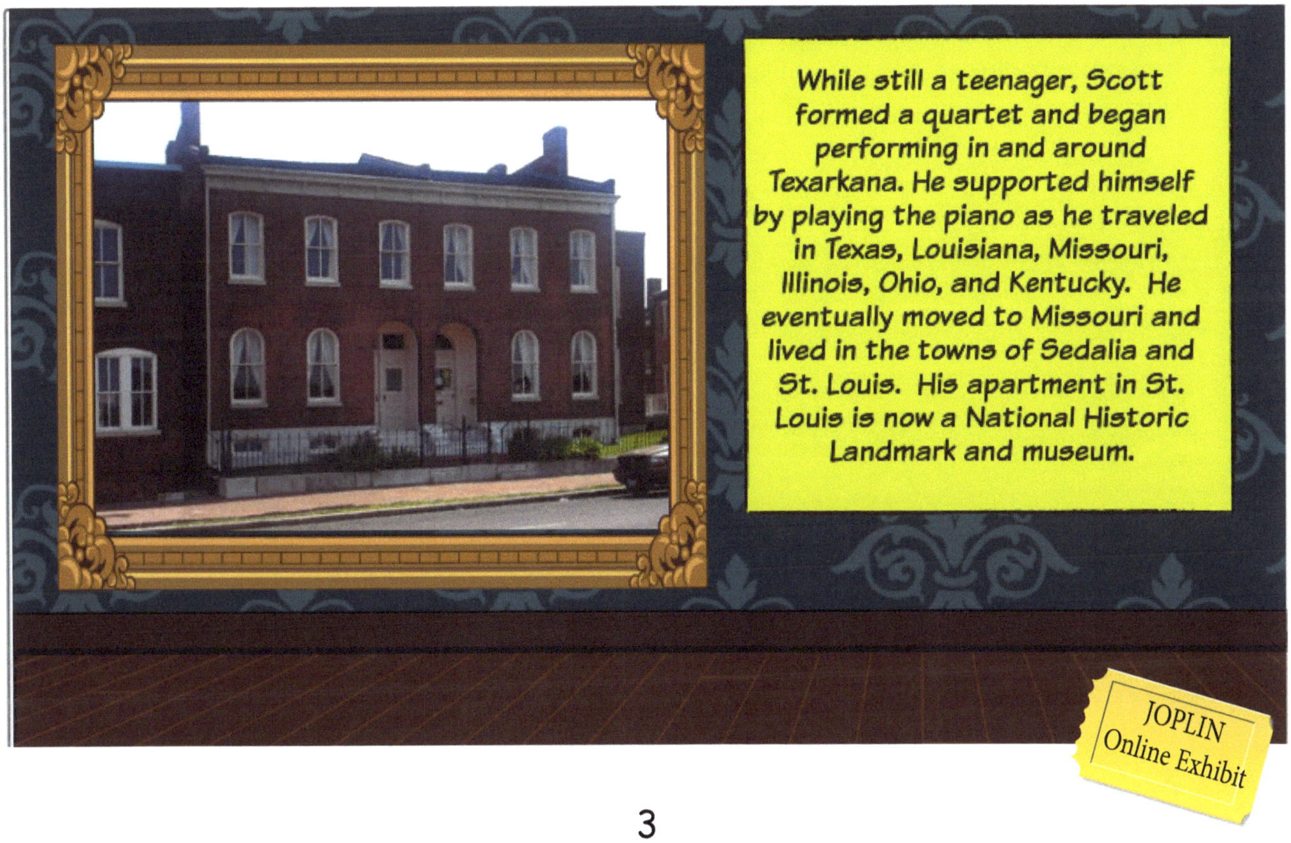

While still a teenager, Scott formed a quartet and began performing in and around Texarkana. He supported himself by playing the piano as he traveled in Texas, Louisiana, Missouri, Illinois, Ohio, and Kentucky. He eventually moved to Missouri and lived in the towns of Sedalia and St. Louis. His apartment in St. Louis is now a National Historic Landmark and museum.

JOPLIN Online Exhibit

People loved his music! John Philip Sousa's band played Mr. Joplin's music, too. The "Maple Leaf Rag" was a big hit across the nation, eventually selling over one million copies!

Mr. Joplin valued the music education he received and shared his talent through teaching. He was considered a hero to the young piano players.

JOPLIN Online Exhibit

Like all of us, Mr. Joplin's life was filled with both joy and sorrow. His only child, a daughter, died when she was only a few months old. A short time later, Scott and his wife Belle drifted apart.

JOPLIN Online Exhibit

Mr. Joplin always wanted to write serious music as well as popular tunes. In 1903, he wrote his first opera, *A Guest of Honor*, and began a tour with about 30 performers.

He never lived in any one place very long. He traveled a lot, sometimes by himself, sometimes with a band or group he formed. He played for money and helped sell his music that was already in print.

JOPLIN Online Exhibit

Mr. Joplin dedicated "The Chrysanthemum" to Freddie Alexander, a young woman from Arkansas. They were married in June 1904, but she became ill and died just ten weeks later.

His first copyrighted song after Freddie's death was "Bethena." He dedicated the song to the couple who helped him through the difficult days following Freddie's death.

JOPLIN Online Exhibit

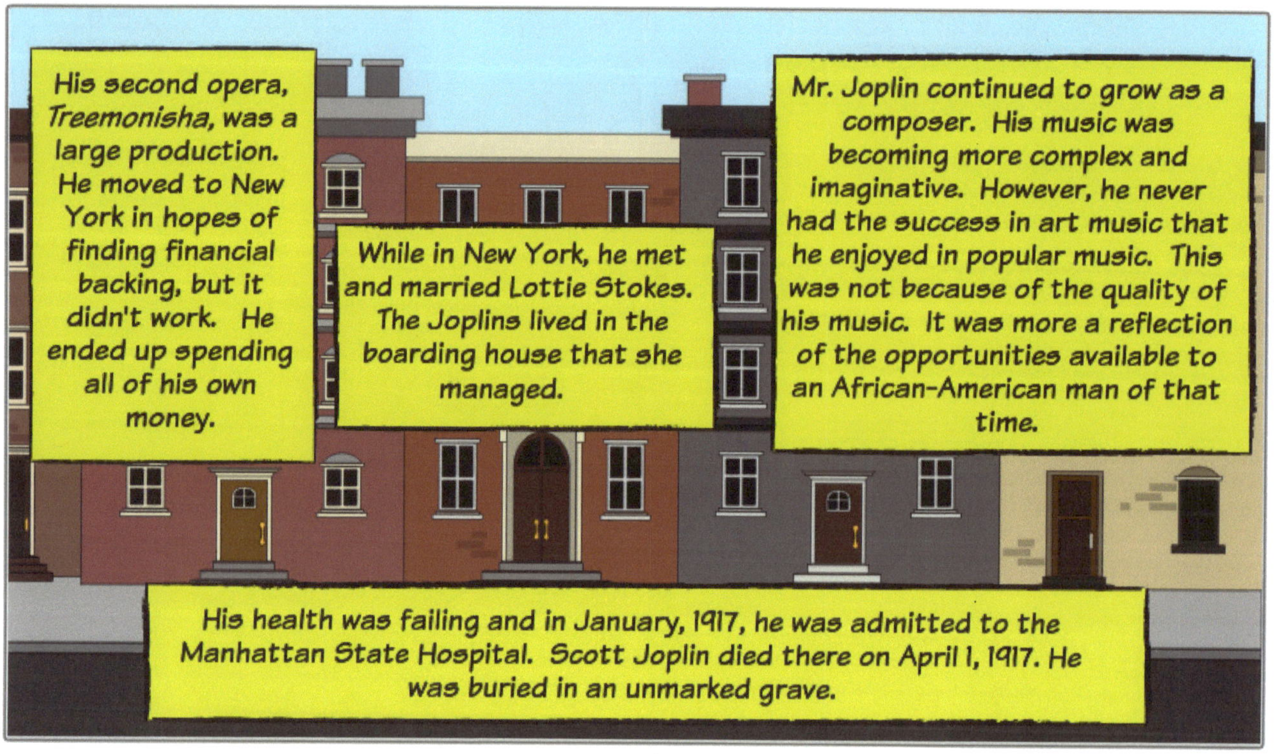

His second opera, *Treemonisha*, was a large production. He moved to New York in hopes of finding financial backing, but it didn't work. He ended up spending all of his own money.

While in New York, he met and married Lottie Stokes. The Joplins lived in the boarding house that she managed.

Mr. Joplin continued to grow as a composer. His music was becoming more complex and imaginative. However, he never had the success in art music that he enjoyed in popular music. This was not because of the quality of his music. It was more a reflection of the opportunities available to an African-American man of that time.

His health was failing and in January, 1917, he was admitted to the Manhattan State Hospital. Scott Joplin died there on April 1, 1917. He was buried in an unmarked grave.

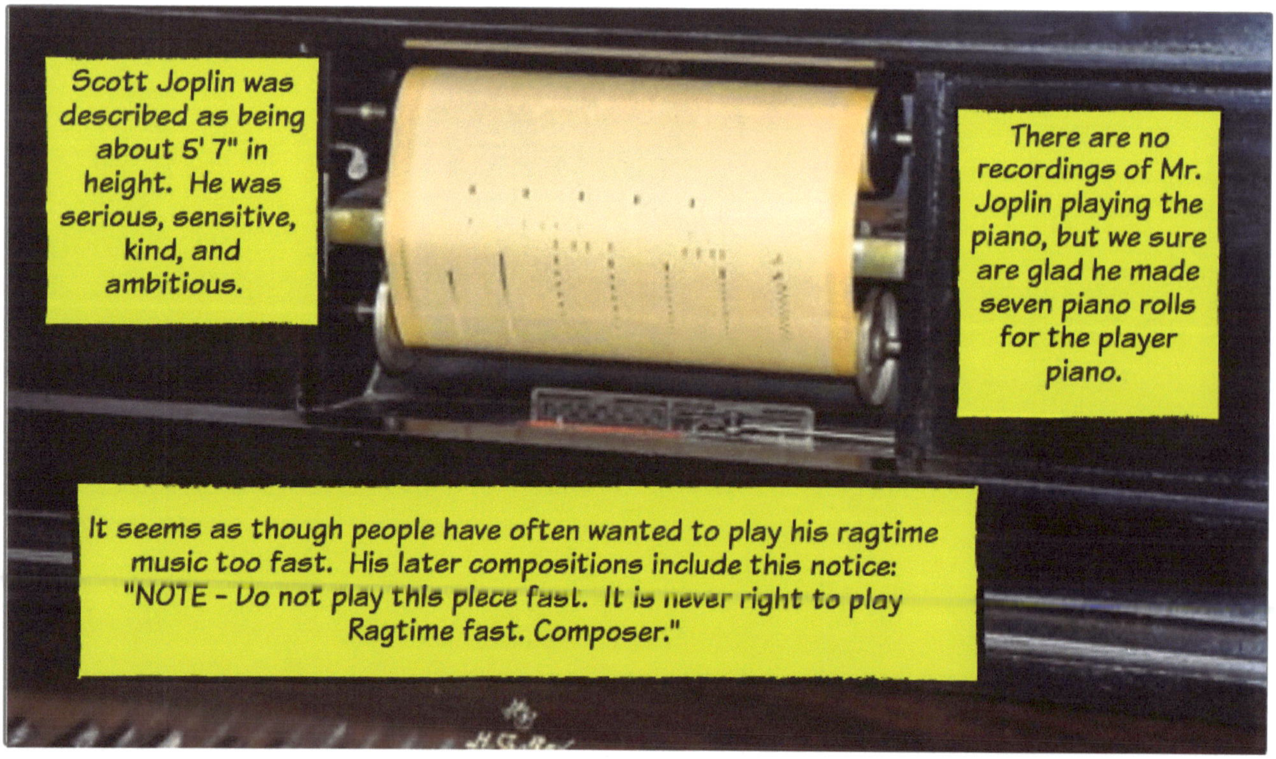

Scott Joplin was described as being about 5' 7" in height. He was serious, sensitive, kind, and ambitious.

There are no recordings of Mr. Joplin playing the piano, but we sure are glad he made seven piano rolls for the player piano.

It seems as though people have often wanted to play his ragtime music too fast. His later compositions include this notice: "NOTE – Do not play this piece fast. It is never right to play Ragtime fast. Composer."

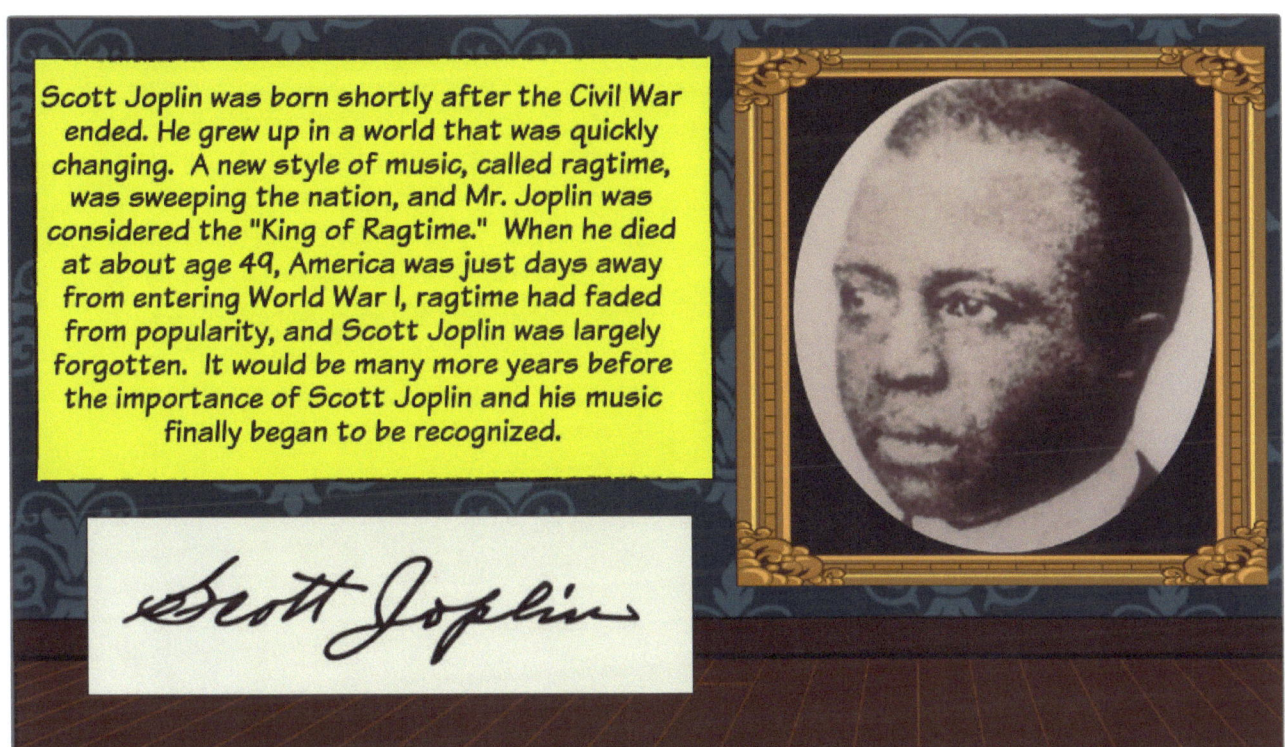

Maple Leaf Rag FAQ

People LOVE Mr. Joplin's song called "Maple Leaf Rag," but sometimes in telling the story about how the song came to be, the truth gets mixed up with the legend.

A lot of people write to us and ask interesting questions. Let's look through these letters and see if we can sort some of this out.

I know he is called the "King of Ragtime Writers," but did Scott Joplin invent ragtime music?

No, he didn't invent ragtime. What Mr. Joplin did was to raise it to a whole new level and perfect it. "Maple Leaf Rag" is one of his masterpieces! Other composers copied his form and style, but Scott Joplin was the king!

Is "Maple Leaf Rag" his most popular song?

It depends on whom you ask! Today, people are probably more familiar with "The Entertainer" since it was heard in the 1973 film, *The Sting*. In Mr. Joplin's time, however, "Maple Leaf Rag" was by far his most popular song.

I heard that the "Maple Leaf Rag" was named for the Maple Leaf Club in Sedalia, Missouri. Is that true?

Possibly. There was a men's group called the Maple Leaf Club when Mr. Joplin lived in Sedalia, and he did play the piano in a building called the Maple Leaf. The club meetings were held in that building for a short time. We don't know for sure if the song was named for the club or the building. The building was demolished many years ago.

JOPLIN Online Exhibit

When did Mr. Joplin write "Maple Leaf Rag"?

Well, we don't know that for sure either, but people heard it in Sedalia before it was seen in print.

It was published by John Stark in 1899. Mr. Stark owned a music store and was a music publisher in Sedalia. There are several versions of the story about how Mr. Joplin and Mr. Stark got together, but however it happened, the important point is that they did! They worked together on a lot of songs.

At that time in history, black composers typically sold their songs for a small, one-time payment. Mr. Stark and Mr. Joplin worked out a deal which was very fair for both of them. Mr. Joplin received a royalty of one cent for every copy that sold. That may not sound like a lot, but it gave him an income for the rest of his life! Sales were slow at first, but "Maple Leaf Rag" became a best seller across the nation.

Mr. Joplin was never rich but made enough money that he could finally focus his creativity on writing other types of music.

Was "Maple Leaf Rag" played on the Titanic?

Maybe. It was included in the White Star Line songbook, but we will never know if it was played on the Titanic's first -- and last -- voyage.

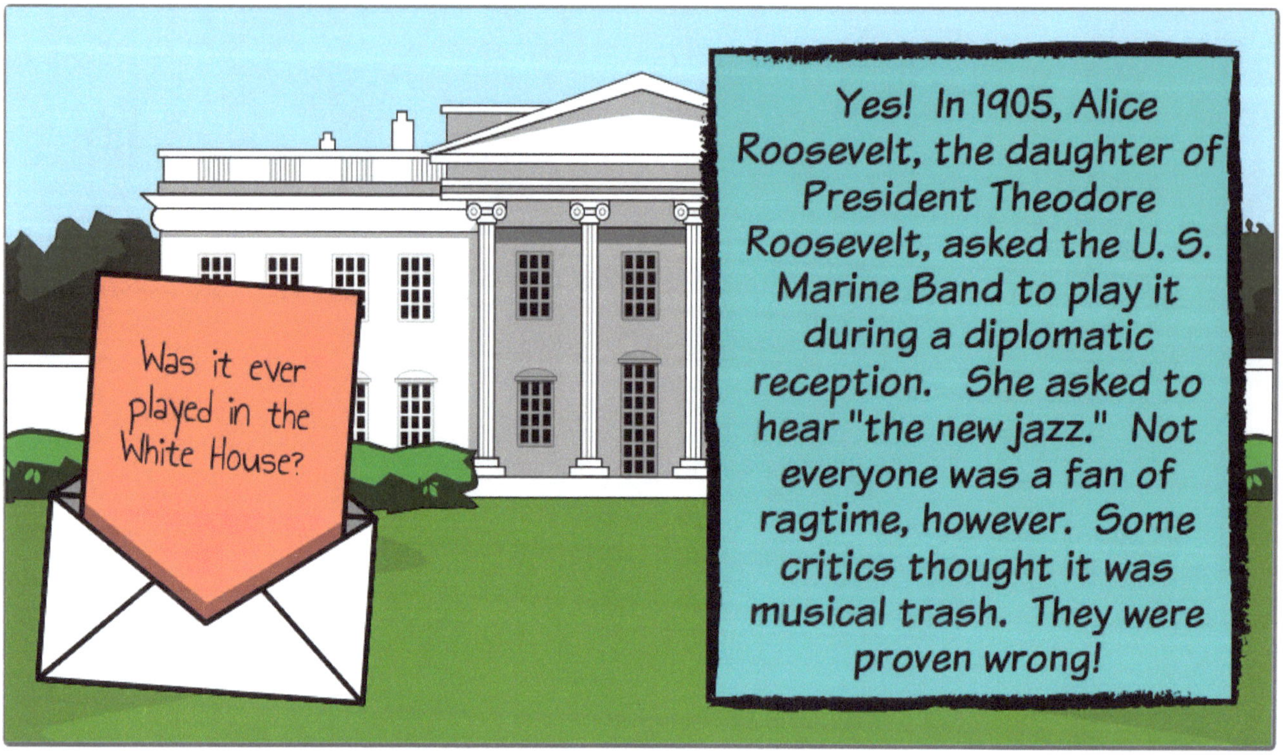

Was it ever played in the White House?

Yes! In 1905, Alice Roosevelt, the daughter of President Theodore Roosevelt, asked the U. S. Marine Band to play it during a diplomatic reception. She asked to hear "the new jazz." Not everyone was a fan of ragtime, however. Some critics thought it was musical trash. They were proven wrong!

Did Scott Joplin play "Maple Leaf Rag" at the Columbian Exposition in Chicago (World's Fair)?

No. The fair was in 1893, a few years before he published "Maple Leaf Rag." Mr. Joplin and his band were in Chicago during the Exposition, but black musicians were not part of the entertainment inside the fairgrounds. Instead, they played music in many nearby places. The fair played an important role in making ragtime music very popular and in gaining national recognition.

Did he ever make a recording of "Maple Leaf Rag"?

There are no true recordings of Mr. Joplin performing. However, it is believed he made a few piano rolls. One of them from 1916 is "Maple Leaf Rag." Sadly, by then his health was failing and many mistakes can be heard.

He wanted "Maple Leaf Rag" played at his funeral. His wife thought it was inappropriate for a funeral and didn't follow his wishes. She later regretted that decision.

JOPLIN Online Exhibit

Oh, I LOVE all of these questions!

I still have some work to do, so you go on ahead and read more about Mr. Joplin and his music. It was nice to meet you!

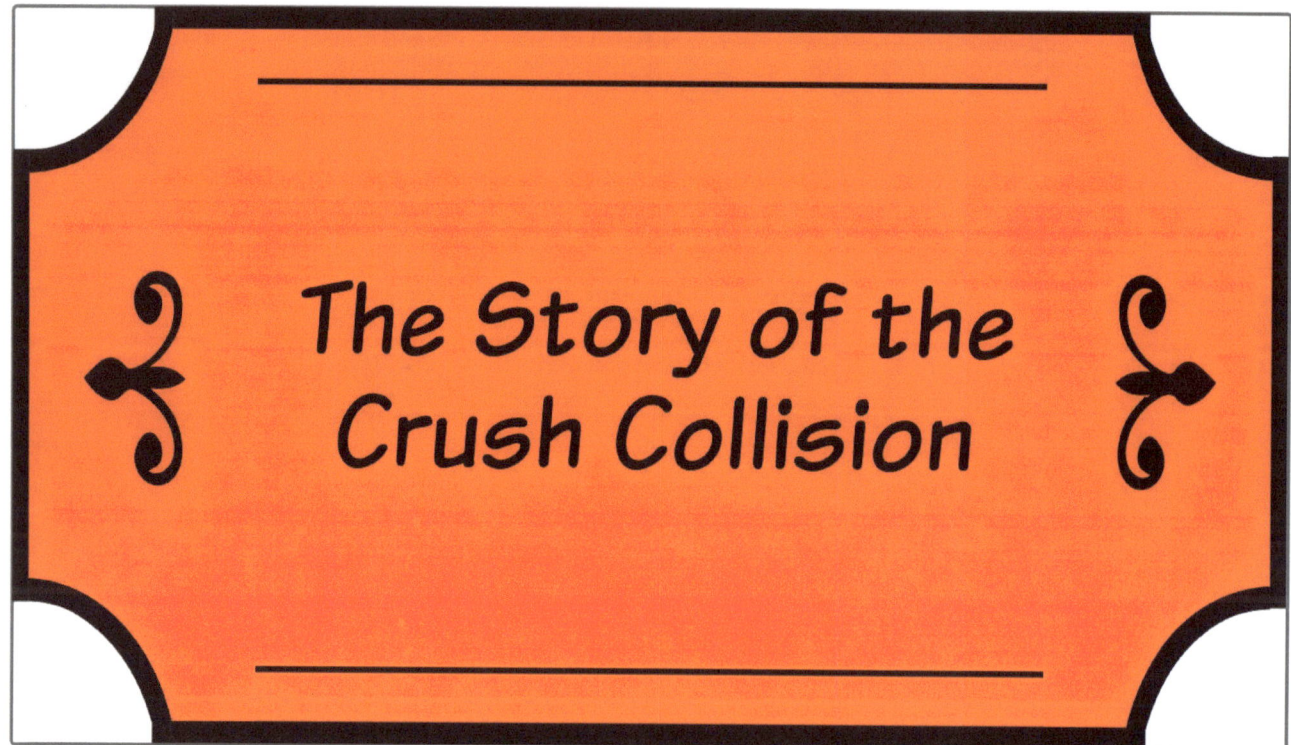

Howdy! I'm glad you stopped by. Pull up a log and sit a spell. They call me Old Jack, and I'm going to tell you the TRUE story of one man's wild idea...and how it went very, very wrong.

Our story takes place in September of 1896, near Waco, Texas, in a small town called West. There was a man, William George Crush by name, who worked for the Missouri-Kansas-Texas Railroad Company (but around here we just call it the "Katy".)

Well, that Mr. Crush got the notion that he should stage a publicity stunt. He decided to make up a new town for the occasion and he called it Crush. Now that right there should be a clue that things are not going to end well, don't you think?

His plan was to take two old locomotives and run them into each other, a head-on collision at full steam!

And you know what? His bosses AGREED to it because they thought they would make money from all the people who would buy tickets to come and watch. This really is getting scary!

15

Some reports said about 40,000 people came to Crush that day. That was one BIG party! The two locomotives sat nose to nose with six boxcars behind each engine. At five o'clock they began to back up until they were one mile apart. Then they started moving toward each other, slowly at first, then faster and faster. The train whistles blew and the engineers jumped off.

The trains collided, the boilers exploded, and people panicked and ran. Two or three people were killed and others badly hurt. What a tragedy!

Even MORE people were hurt as they ran to pick up souvenirs from the wreckage. What were they thinking?!?! Some of those metal chunks were sharp as knives and fire hot!

I reckon you won't be surprised to find out that Mr. Crush got fired right after the collision.

But you know what? Since the company made a lot of money from the stunt, they hired him back the VERY NEXT DAY!

So there you go, the weird but true story of the collision at Crush.

JOPLIN Online Exhibit

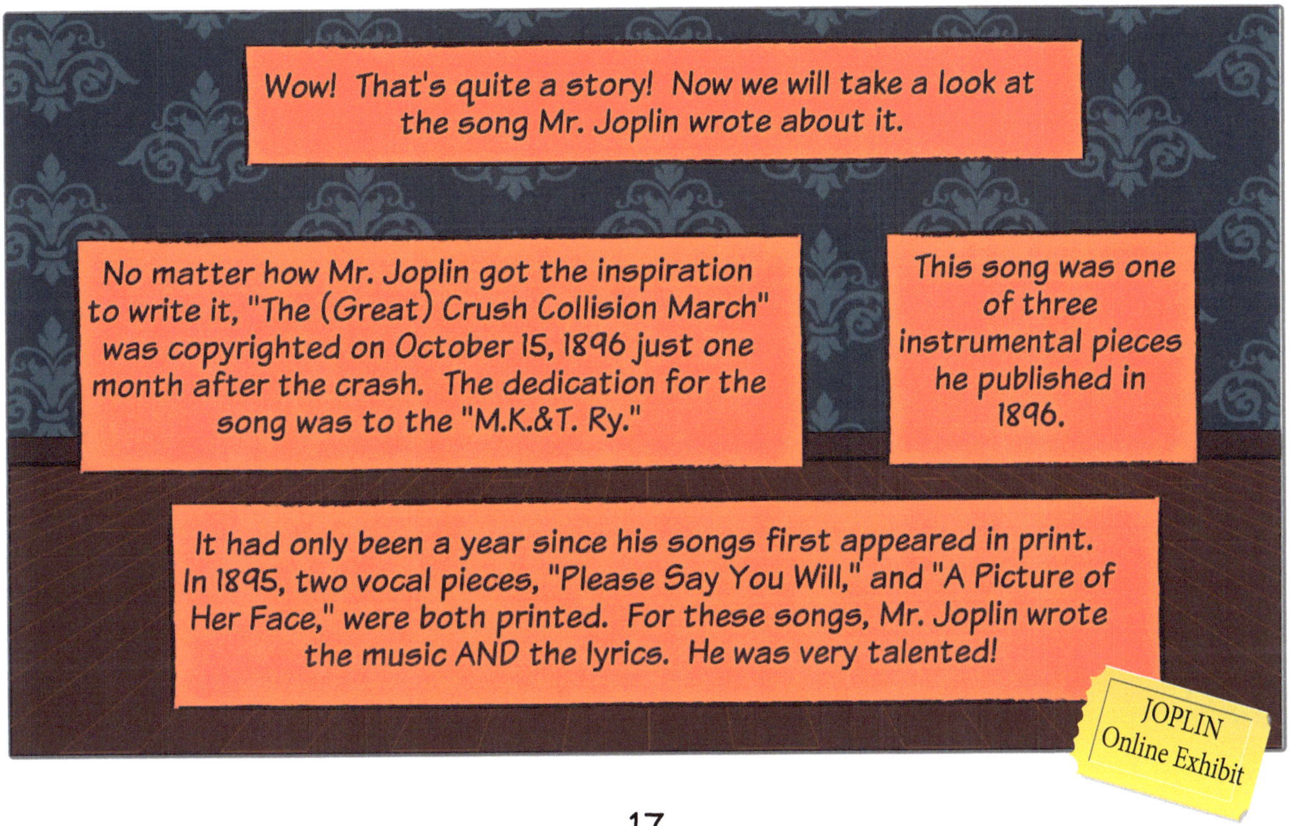

Wow! That's quite a story! Now we will take a look at the song Mr. Joplin wrote about it.

No matter how Mr. Joplin got the inspiration to write it, "The (Great) Crush Collision March" was copyrighted on October 15, 1896 just one month after the crash. The dedication for the song was to the "M.K.&T. Ry."

This song was one of three instrumental pieces he published in 1896.

It had only been a year since his songs first appeared in print. In 1895, two vocal pieces, "Please Say You Will," and "A Picture of Her Face," were both printed. For these songs, Mr. Joplin wrote the music AND the lyrics. He was very talented!

JOPLIN Online Exhibit

In both classical art music and popular instrumental music of this era, composers sometimes included program notes or written description to tell the audience and performers what was happening in the music.

Let's take a look at the interlude of this song and read what Mr. Joplin wants us to imagine happening in this section.

Here is the interlude with Mr. Joplin's notes.

The noises of the trains while running at the rate of sixty miles per hour,

Whistling for the crossing,

Noise of the trains

Whistle before the collision

The collision

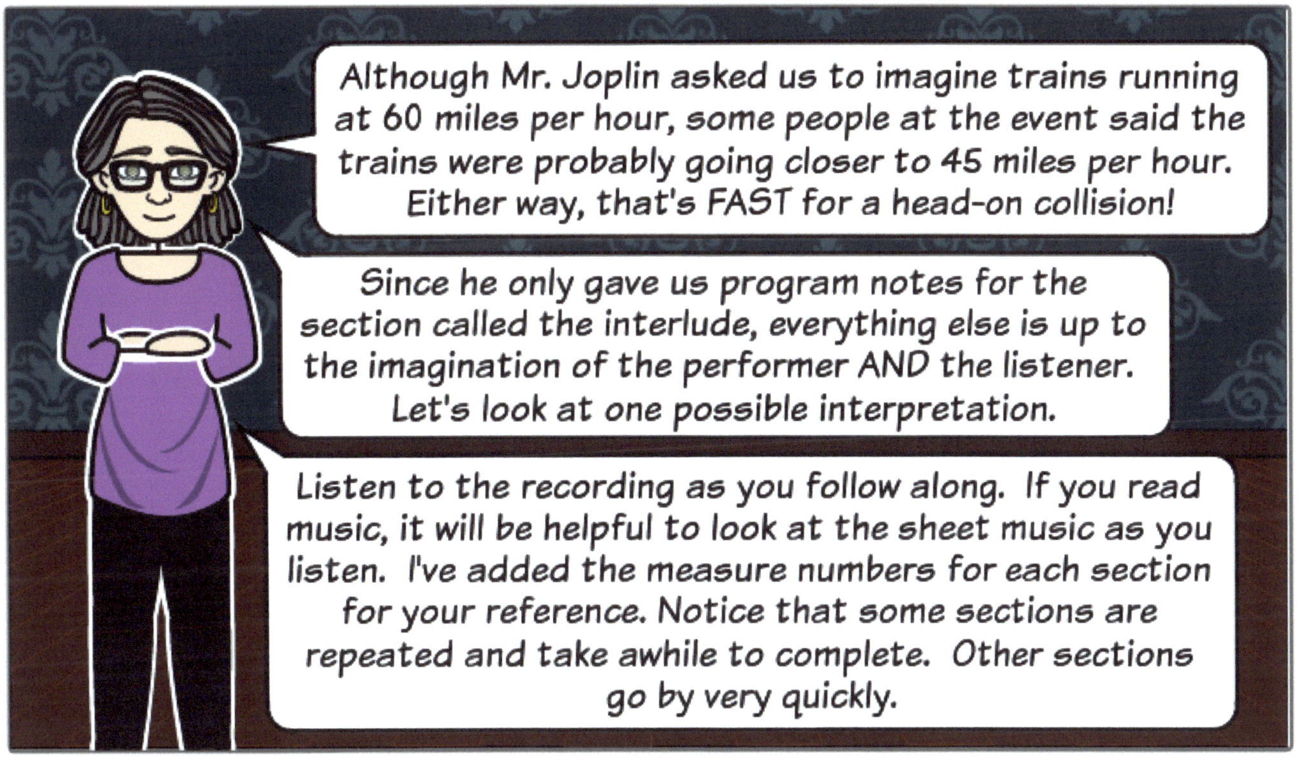

Although Mr. Joplin asked us to imagine trains running at 60 miles per hour, some people at the event said the trains were probably going closer to 45 miles per hour. Either way, that's FAST for a head-on collision!

Since he only gave us program notes for the section called the interlude, everything else is up to the imagination of the performer AND the listener. Let's look at one possible interpretation.

Listen to the recording as you follow along. If you read music, it will be helpful to look at the sheet music as you listen. I've added the measure numbers for each section for your reference. Notice that some sections are repeated and take awhile to complete. Other sections go by very quickly.

The publicity stunt at Crush, Texas September 15, 1896

Introduction
(measures 1-4)

Oh, no! Peril lies ahead!

Theme A
(measures 5-21, repeat)

The dangerous stage is set.

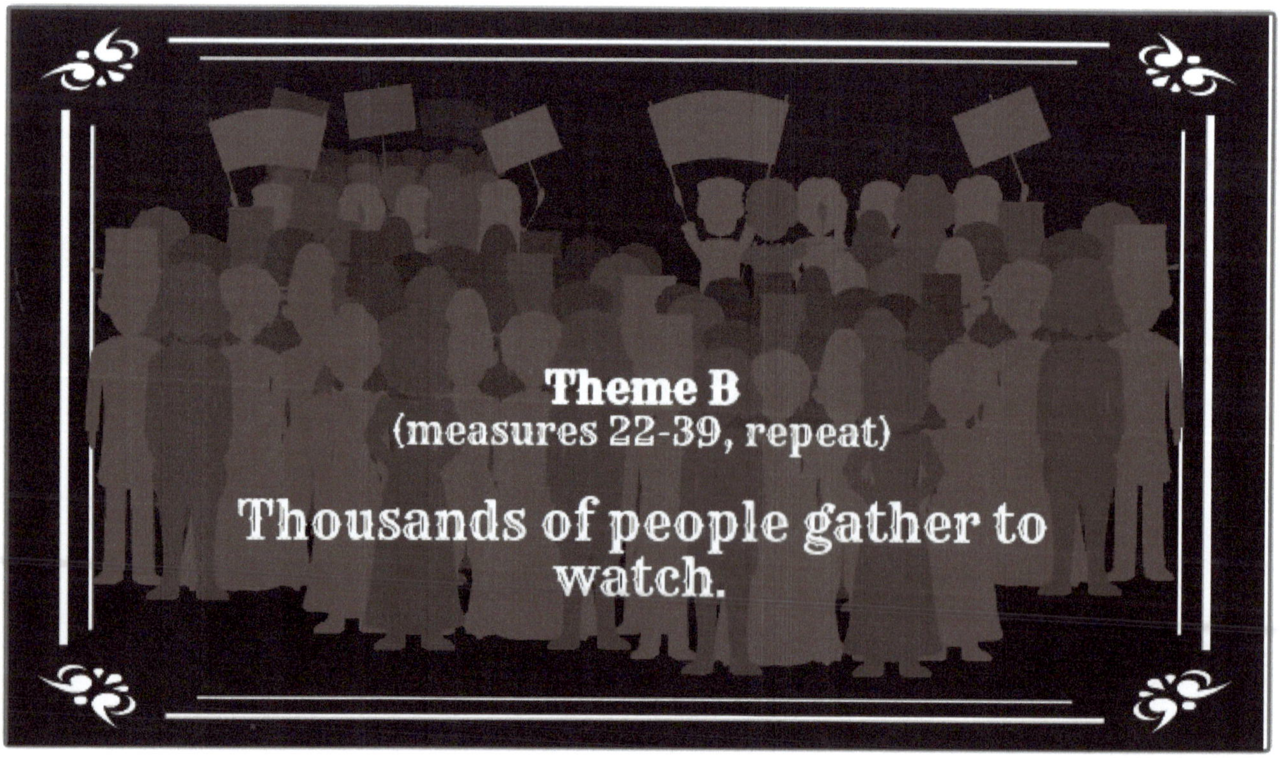

Theme B
(measures 22-39, repeat)

Thousands of people gather to watch.

Theme C
(measures 49-56, repeat)

There is excitement in the air!

Theme D, Trio
(measures 57-73, repeat)

Let's have a PARTY while we wait!

Interlude
(measures 74-81)

The engines are backing up.
The tension builds!

(measures 82-83)

"The noise of the trains while running at the rate of sixty miles per hour,"

(measures 84-85)

"Whistling for the crossing,"

(measures 86-87)

"Noise of the trains,"

(measures 88-89)

"Whistle before the collision,"

CRASH!

(measure 89)

"The collision"

Theme D
(measures 90-106)

The party is over.
Let's get our souvenirs and go home!

In his music, Mr. Joplin instructed us to repeat from the interlude to the end of the song. This is in keeping with the style of his day for writing this type of song. However, some performers do not repeat this section so that the trains only crash once!

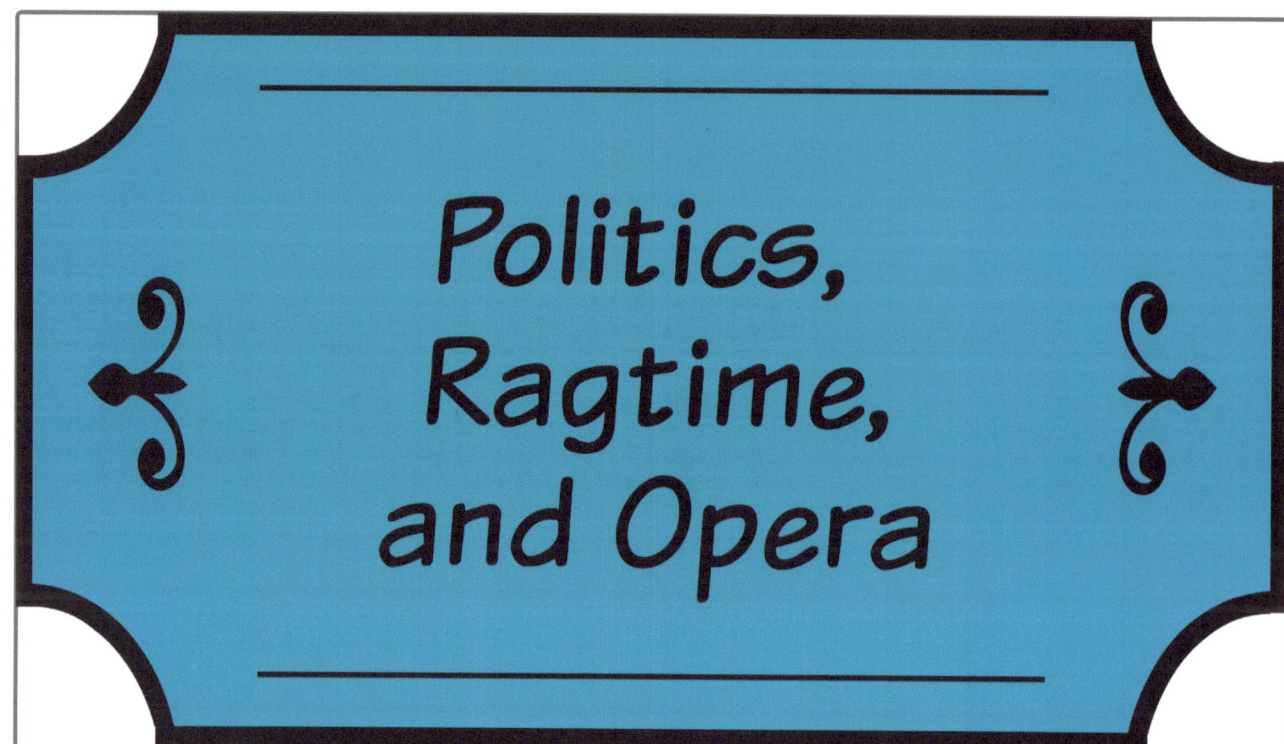

Politics, Ragtime, and Opera

Mr. Joplin wrote about many things that were important to him, including politics!

In 1899, Governor of New York Theodore Roosevelt gave a speech in Chicago, Illinois, called "The Strenuous Life." It was about the importance of hard work and overcoming difficult circumstances. Mr. Joplin certainly understood those ideas! He wrote a song in the form of a two-step rag and gave it the same title as the speech, "The Strenuous Life."

Theodore Roosevelt

JOPLIN Online Exhibit

Shortly after becoming president in 1901, Mr. Roosevelt took a giant step forward for civil rights when he invited Booker T. Washington to dinner at the White House.

Booker T. Washington

While some people severely criticized Roosevelt for doing this, other praised him.

Mr. Joplin felt the event was so important to history that he wrote about it in his first opera, A Guest of Honor.

I know what to do! Music will help people understand the story of President Roosevelt and Mr. Washington!

He was very brave to tell a story that was so full of controversy. His genius was using what he called "rag time opera" to tell that story.

In 1903, Mr. Joplin filed a copyright application for the opera. Copies of the music were usually submitted with the application forms, but for whatever reason, this time the music was not turned in.

Scott Joplin's Ragtime Opera Company begn touring the midwest and gave a few performances.

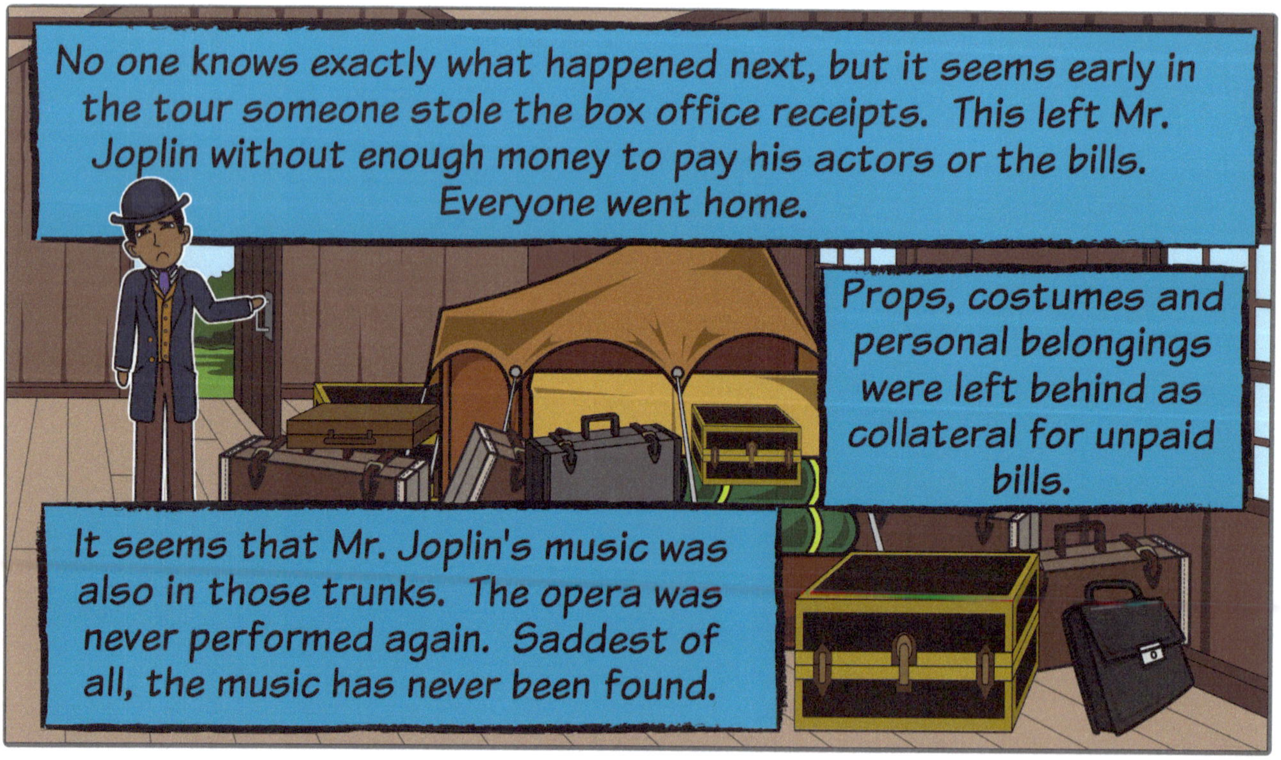

No one knows exactly what happened next, but it seems early in the tour someone stole the box office receipts. This left Mr. Joplin without enough money to pay his actors or the bills. Everyone went home.

Props, costumes and personal belongings were left behind as collateral for unpaid bills.

It seems that Mr. Joplin's music was also in those trunks. The opera was never performed again. Saddest of all, the music has never been found.

Treemonisha and Heartbreak

Beginning in the late 19th century, many of the major music publishing companies were located in a section of New York City called Tin Pan Alley. In 1907, Mr. Joplin rented a home just one block away. John Stark had moved to New York, too, and had his publishing business nearby.

Mr. Joplin was still writing ragtime, and his music was getting better and better. However, his #1 goal was to be known as a classical composer, and to do that, he knew he had to write AND publish more than ragtime.

Shortly after Freddie died, he began work on a very ambitious project, his second opera, called *Treemonisha*. During this time, he also wrote other songs and played the piano just to pay the bills. He poured his heart and soul into his opera work.

Mr. Joplin recognized the need to create African-American art music, and he knew he was uniquely qualified to do it. It was very hard work, and he did it all. He wrote the story, the music, and even the stage directions!

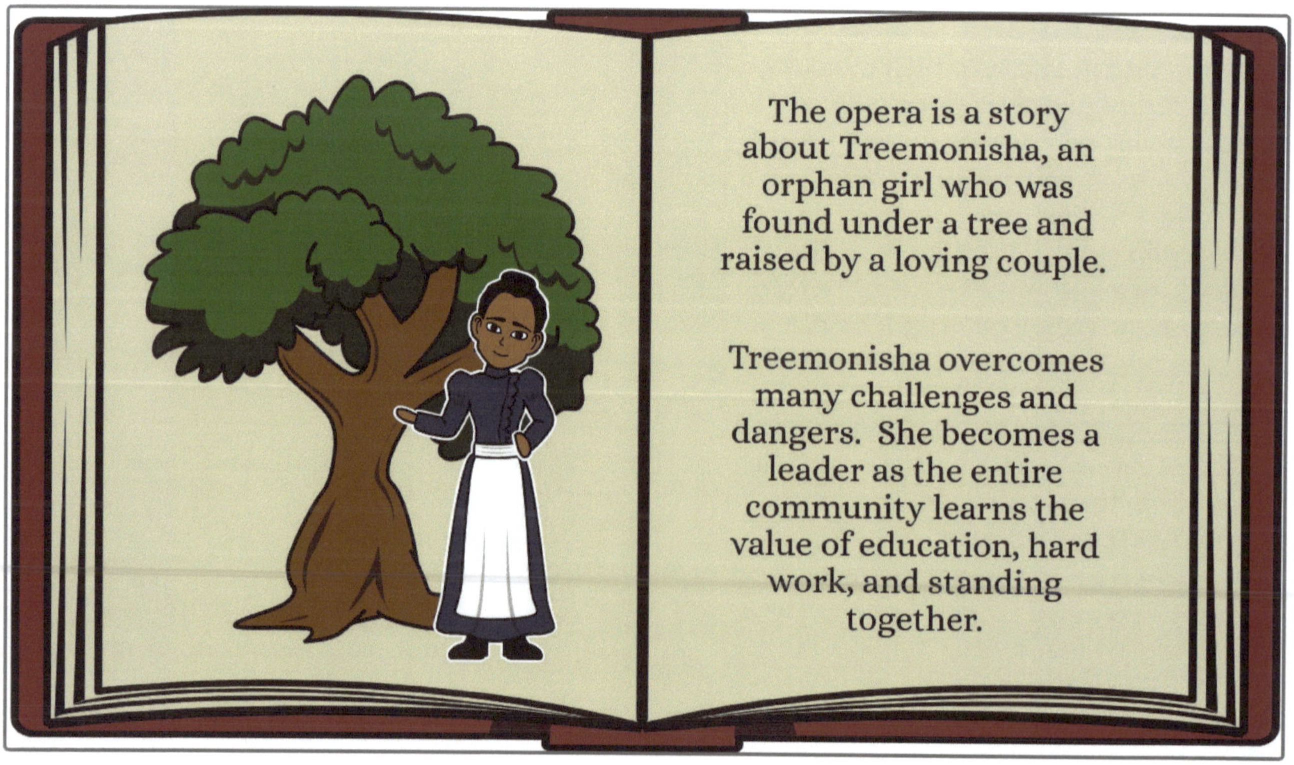

The opera is a story about Treemonisha, an orphan girl who was found under a tree and raised by a loving couple.

Treemonisha overcomes many challenges and dangers. She becomes a leader as the entire community learns the value of education, hard work, and standing together.

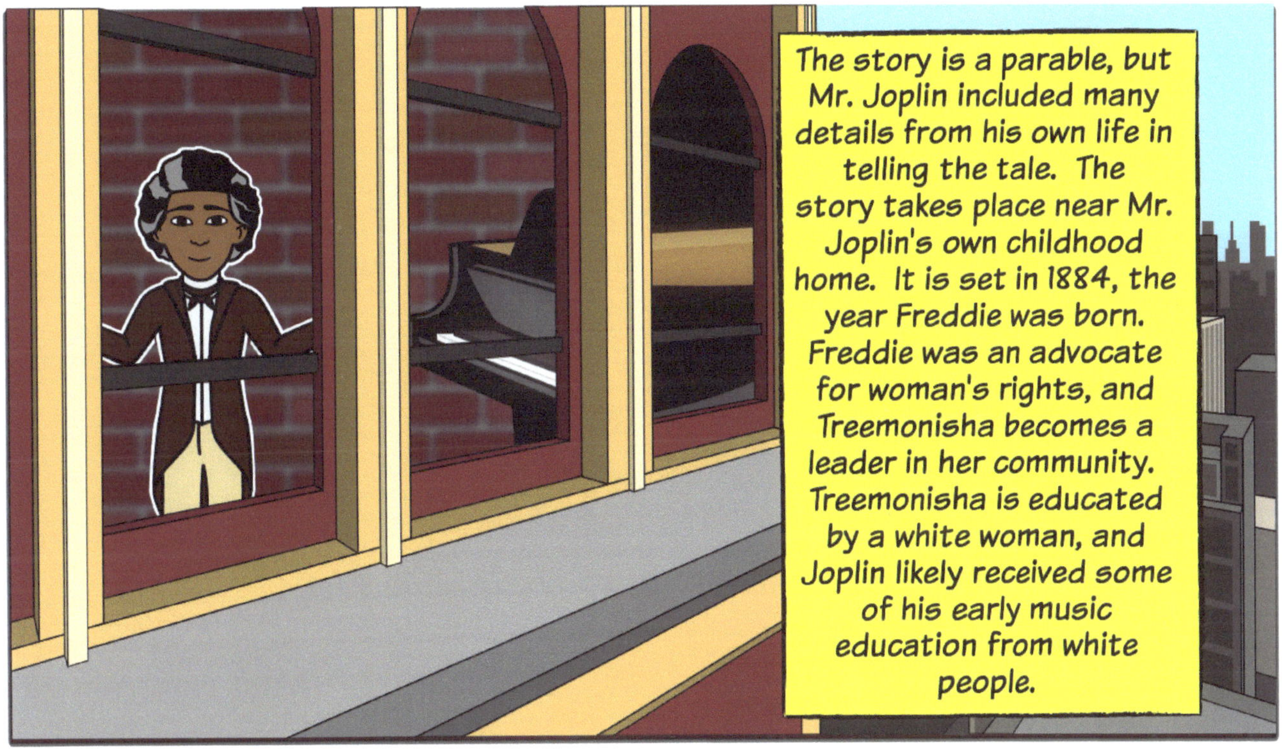

The story is a parable, but Mr. Joplin included many details from his own life in telling the tale. The story takes place near Mr. Joplin's own childhood home. It is set in 1884, the year Freddie was born. Freddie was an advocate for woman's rights, and Treemonisha becomes a leader in her community. Treemonisha is educated by a white woman, and Joplin likely received some of his early music education from white people.

Mr. Joplin first wrote the entire opera in vocal-piano form. Unable to find someone willing to publish it, he finally did so at his own expense. He continued to look for a publisher.

Very discouraged, in 1915 he organized and paid for an expensive full-length performance and played the entire piano accompaniment himself. Even with an invited audience, no financial backer could be found.

He had sacrificed so much to create *Treemonisha* yet never saw it fully staged.

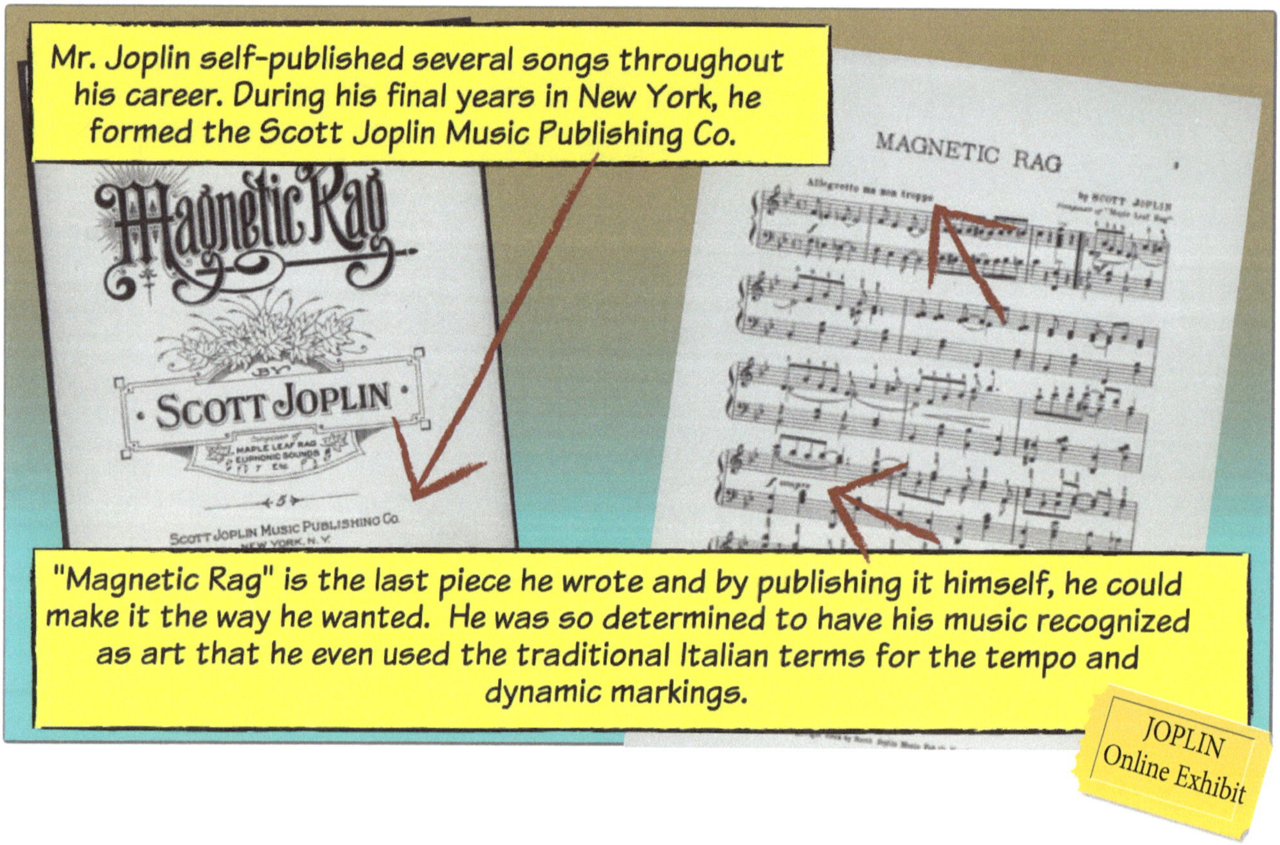

Mr. Joplin self-published several songs throughout his career. During his final years in New York, he formed the Scott Joplin Music Publishing Co.

"Magnetic Rag" is the last piece he wrote and by publishing it himself, he could make it the way he wanted. He was so determined to have his music recognized as art that he even used the traditional Italian terms for the tempo and dynamic markings.

JOPLIN Online Exhibit

These were sad, dark days for Mr. Joplin. He was struggling wih the repeated rejections of *Treemonisha*, his money was gone and his health was failing.

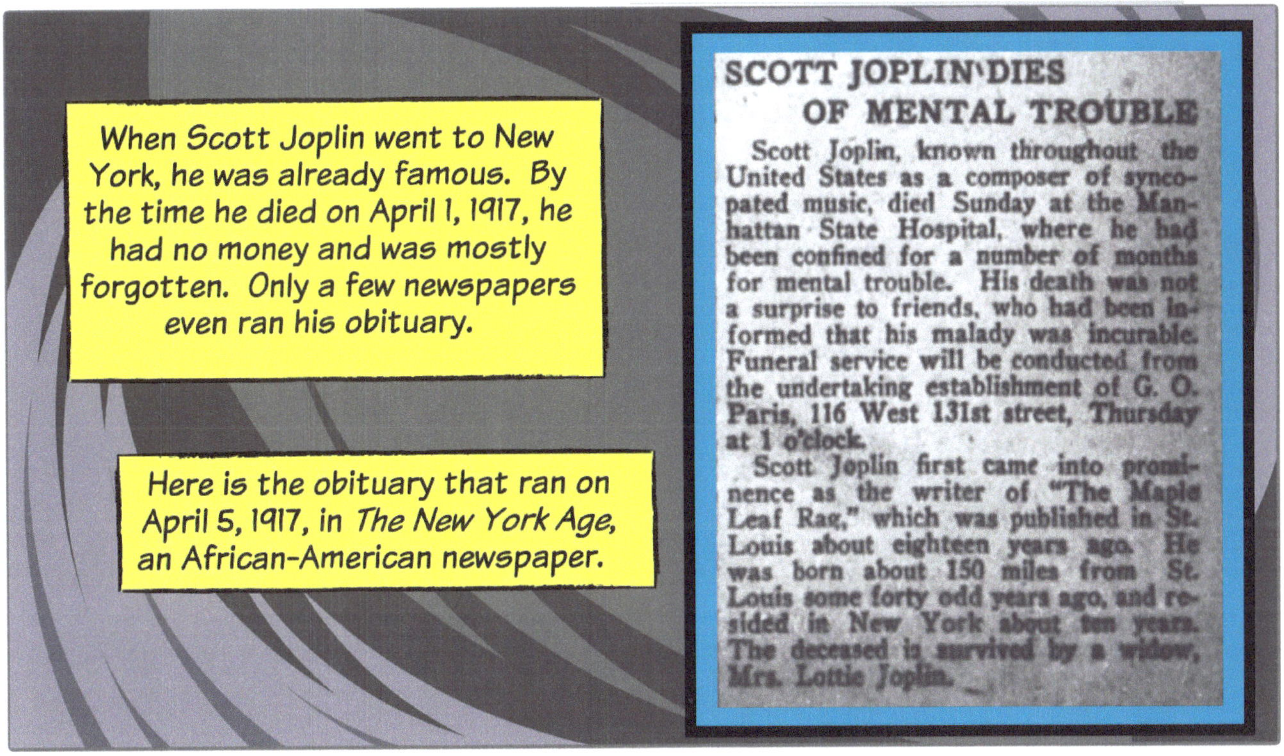

When Scott Joplin went to New York, he was already famous. By the time he died on April 1, 1917, he had no money and was mostly forgotten. Only a few newspapers even ran his obituary.

Here is the obituary that ran on April 5, 1917, in *The New York Age*, an African-American newspaper.

SCOTT JOPLIN DIES OF MENTAL TROUBLE

Scott Joplin, known throughout the United States as a composer of syncopated music, died Sunday at the Manhattan State Hospital, where he had been confined for a number of months for mental trouble. His death was not a surprise to friends, who had been informed that his malady was incurable. Funeral service will be conducted from the undertaking establishment of G. O. Paris, 116 West 131st street, Thursday at 1 o'clock.

Scott Joplin first came into prominence as the writer of "The Maple Leaf Rag," which was published in St. Louis about eighteen years ago. He was born about 150 miles from St. Louis some forty odd years ago, and resided in New York about ten years. The deceased is survived by a widow, Mrs. Lottie Joplin.

Scott Joplin was buried in an unmarked pauper's grave in St. Michael's Cemetery, East Elmhurst, Queens County, New York.

Awards, Memorials, and Legacy

As ragtime faded from popularity, so did the music of Scott Joplin. Jazz and other new music became more fashionable.

But then, finally, in the 1970s, his music started to be heard again when Joshua Rifkin made recordings of Mr. Joplin's piano music. Mr. Joplin always wanted his music to be considered classical (art) music and this is exactly how it was recorded and marketed. The recorded collection has sold over one million copies!

At last! It's about time!

Songwriters Hall of Fame!

The Songwriters Hall of Fame was founded in 1969. In 1970, Scott Joplin was inducted into this list of music greats.

Marvin Hamlisch realized this renewed interest in ragtime made it the perfect music to feature in his score for the 1973 movie, *The Sting*. Much of the music from the movie was based on Mr. Joplin's rags. The most popular of these was "The Entertainer." The movie was nominated for ten Academy Awards and won seven. Hamlisch received the Academy Award for Best Score. But you know what? The movie was set in the 1930s, and by then ragtime really wasn't so popular!

JOPLIN Online Exhibit

In 1974, the Hamlisch version of "The Entertainer" was a top hit, reaching number 3 on the Billboard Hot 100 and American Top 40 charts.

Mr. Joplin had sacrificed so much in his efforts to have *Treemonisha* performed. The complete opera was finally premiered in 1972.

JOPLIN Online Exhibit

In 1976, the Pulitzer Prize was awarded to Scott Joplin for *Treemonisha*. The award read, "A special award is bestowed posthumously on Scott Joplin, in this Bicentennial Year, for his contribution to American Music."

Pulitzer Prize!

In 1974, 57 years after his passing, a marker was placed on his gravesite by ASCAP (American Society of Composers, Authors and Publishers). Sadly, the birthdate on the marker is incorrect.

To mark the 100th anniversary of his death, a memorial bench was placed near the grave. It was paid for with private funds. On the side facing the grave, there is an engraving of the title of a song from his opera *Treemonisha*. The song is "We Will Rest Awhile."

JOPLIN Online Exhibit

In 1976, the Texas Historical Commision placed a marker in Texarakana, Texas, not far from where the Joplin family lived. The marker includes a brief biography.

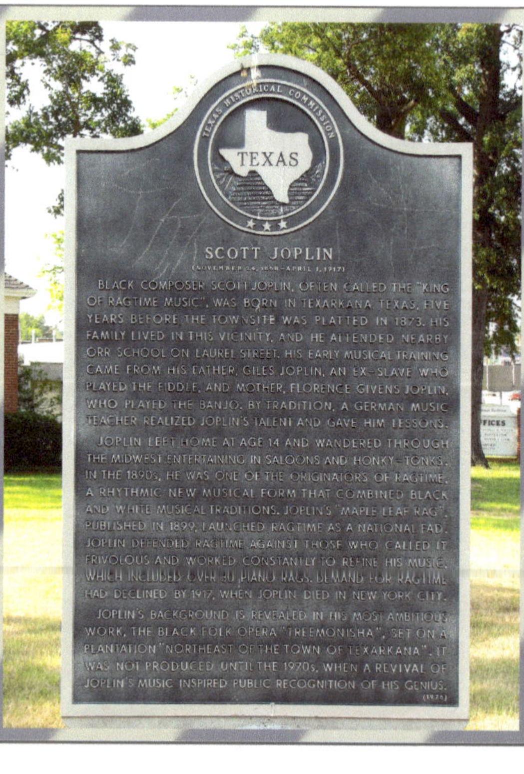

"This is a good place for bird watching!"

Texarakana, Texas, has a 7-acre city park named for Mr. Joplin.

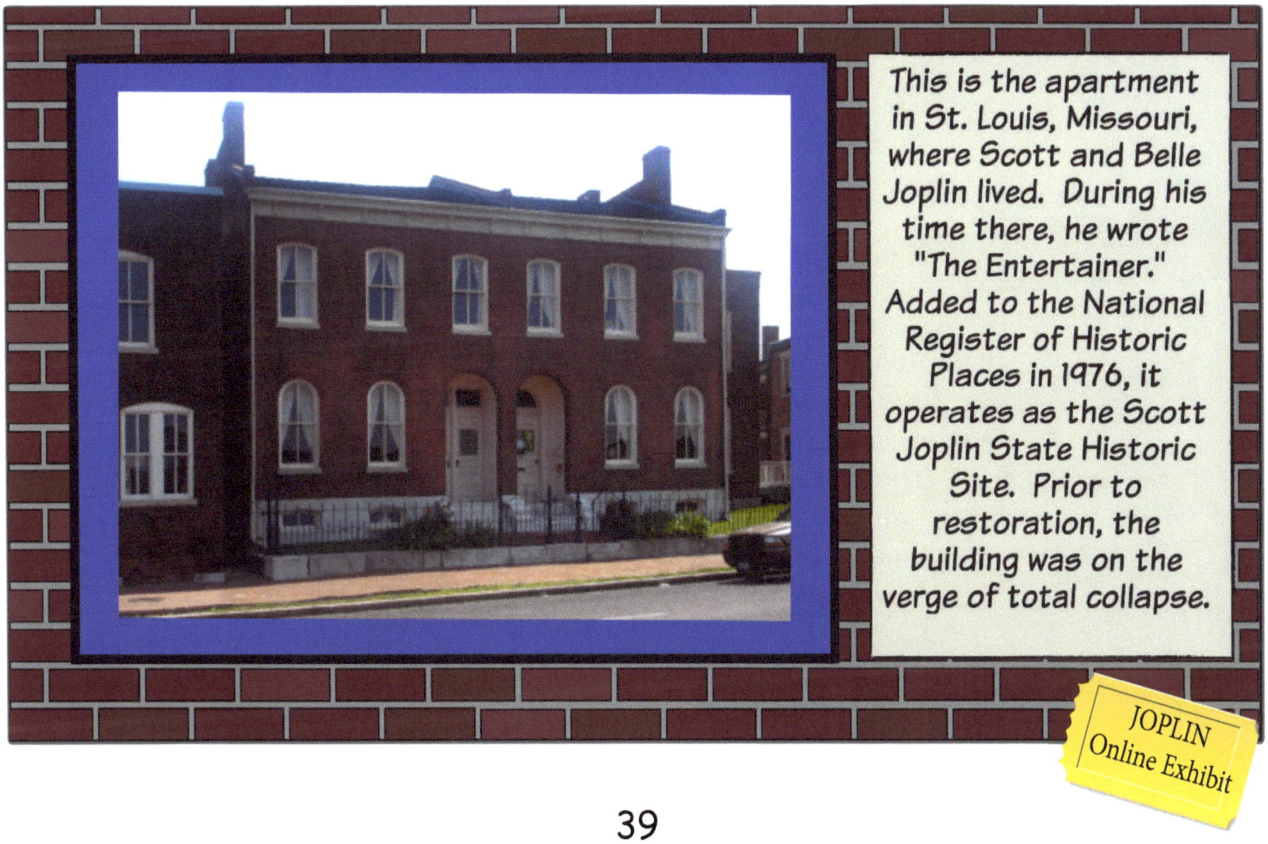

This is the apartment in St. Louis, Missouri, where Scott and Belle Joplin lived. During his time there, he wrote "The Entertainer." Added to the National Register of Historic Places in 1976, it operates as the Scott Joplin State Historic Site. Prior to restoration, the building was on the verge of total collapse.

JOPLIN Online Exhibit

The United States Postal Service honored Mr. Joplin with a 20-cent postage stamp as part of their Black Heritage series. The stamp was issued June 9, 1983, in Sedalia, Missouri. The citizens of Sedalia and fans of ragtime were persistent in their quest for a stamp. It took 10 years from the origination of the idea until the issue of the stamp!

In University City, Missouri, a marker for Scott Joplin is included in the St. Louis Walk of Fame series. It was erected in 1989.

The Scott Joplin International Ragtime Foundation is a nonprofit organization based in Sedalia, Missouri. It states its mission is "to promote an understanding and appreciation of Joplin's contribution to ragtime music, along with the historic importance connected with Sedalia, Missouri." The Scott Joplin International Ragime Music Festival is celebrated every year.

JOPLIN Online Exhibit

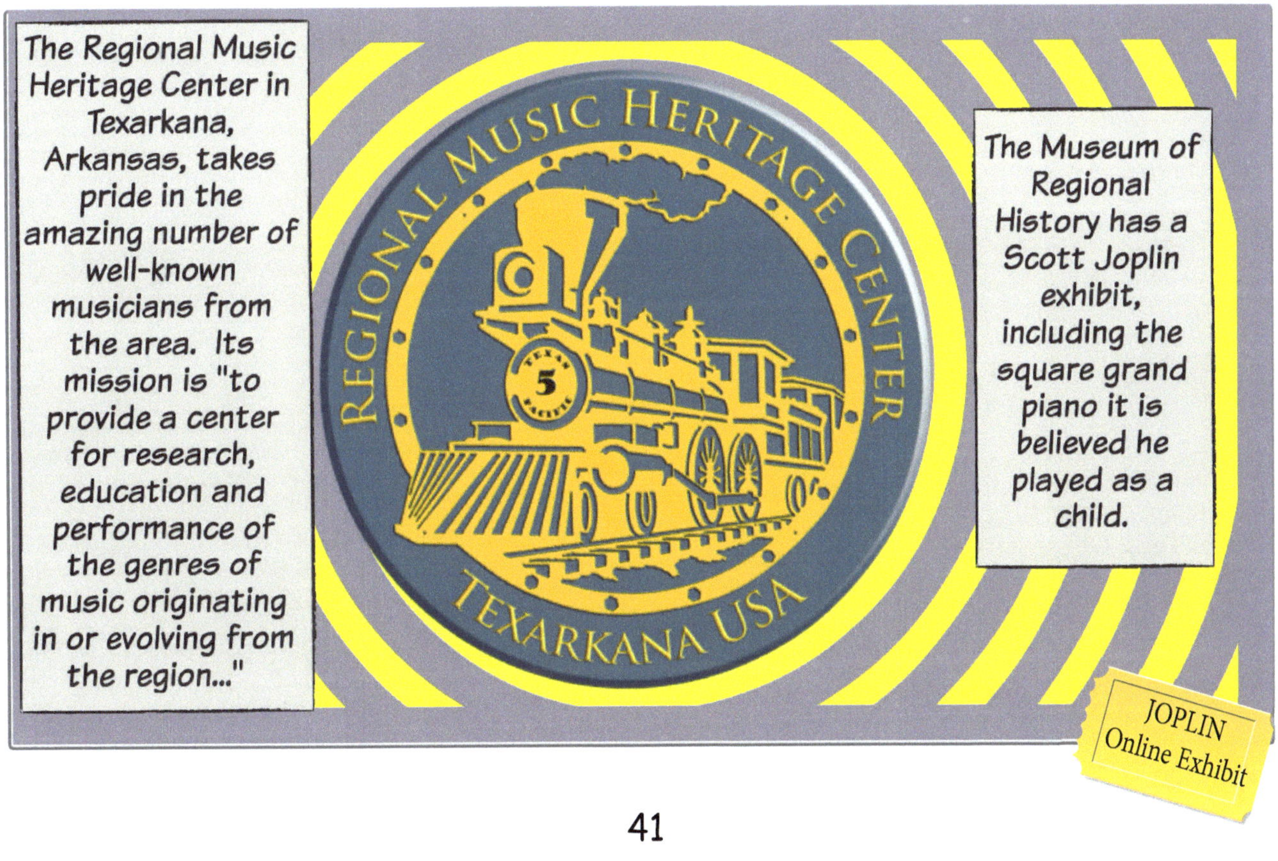

The Regional Music Heritage Center in Texarkana, Arkansas, takes pride in the amazing number of well-known musicians from the area. Its mission is "to provide a center for research, education and performance of the genres of music originating in or evolving from the region..."

The Museum of Regional History has a Scott Joplin exhibit, including the square grand piano it is believed he played as a child.

JOPLIN Online Exhibit

Remember this photo of the Orr School you saw in Mr. Joplin's life story?

The Orr School is located in Texarakana, Arkansas, and was constructed around 1880. It is the only remaining building connected to Scott Joplin in his hometown.

This is how the building looks today. In the early 1920s, the top floor was destroyed by fire, and an extension was added to the back of the building.

JOPLIN Online Exhibit

There are two small plaques, one on each side of the entry door. They designate the site as listed on the National Register of Historic Places and were issued by the United States National Parks Service in 1976.

In 1977, a marker was added by the Association for the Study of Afro-American Life and History.

Texarkana also honors Mr. Joplin with this large mural featuring some of his greatest hits.

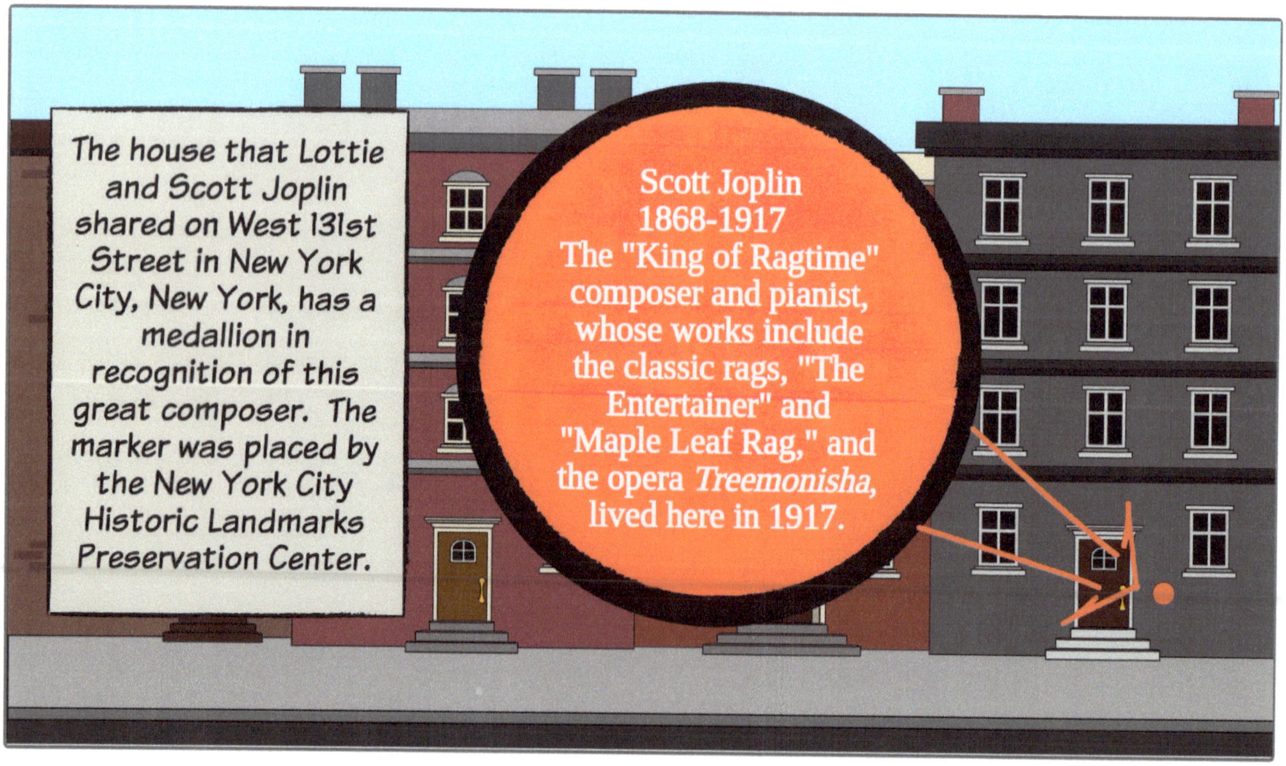

The house that Lottie and Scott Joplin shared on West 131st Street in New York City, New York, has a medallion in recognition of this great composer. The marker was placed by the New York City Historic Landmarks Preservation Center.

Scott Joplin
1868-1917
The "King of Ragtime" composer and pianist, whose works include the classic rags, "The Entertainer" and "Maple Leaf Rag," and the opera *Treemonisha*, lived here in 1917.

It is difficult to read the story of Scott Joplin's life without feeling sad. He worked so hard and suffered such great losses. In his lifetime, he did not receive the recognition he was due.

BUT it is important that we remember him for all he achieved! He developed a new style of music, then never stopped working to share it with everyone. In his lifetime, he wrote 44 ragtime pieces for piano, 2 ragtime operas and several other songs.

The son of an emancipated slave, Scott Joplin was born into a hard-working family in the rural south. There were some good changes to America in the years following the Civil War. Slavery was abolished. Travel was getting easier due to the expansion of the railroad. Many items, including music instruments, were mass-produced making things more affordable.

In spite of many positive changes, however, Mr. Joplin -- and his music -- experienced many hardships and limitations due to his race.

Scott Joplin lived his life with consistency. He worked incredibly hard. He respected his musical heritage and built on it. His music showed true genius. He was commited to ragtime music, taught it to others, and raised it to a true art form. When the "King of Ragtime" died, the ragtime era was over.

Scott Joplin, 1907

Resources and Credits

Bibliography
"Maple Leaf Rag." *American Heritage*, June 1975.

Ayers, Edward. "A New History of the American South." *The Great Courses Plus*, The Teaching Company, 2018.

Berlin, Edward A. *King of Ragtime: Scott Joplin and His Era.* Oxford University Press, 2016.

Blesh, Rudi, and Harriet Grossman. Janis. *They All Played Ragtime.* Oak Publications, 1966.

Editors. "1976 Pulitzer Prizes." *The Pulitzer Prizes*, 2019, www.pulitzer.org/.

Mallette, David. "A Talk About Scott Joplin and His Music." Apr. 2018.

Wildman, Don. "Crash by Crush." *Travel Channel*, 20 Dec. 2012, www.travelchannel.com/videos/crash-by-crush-0197687.

Young, Greg, and Tom Meyers. "Scott Joplin in New York: A Ragtime Mystery." *The Bowery Boys: New York City History*, 23 Feb. 2019, www.boweryboyshistory.com/.

Illustrations
Storyboards created with StoryboardThat. www.storyboardthat.com.

Photo and Artwork Credits
Title page, 2, 8, 47 - "File:Scott Joplin.Jpg - Wikimedia Commons." 2020. Wikimedia.Org. 2020. https://commons.wikimedia.org/wiki/File:Scott_Joplin.jpg.

Page 3, 43 - Orr School, United States Public Domain.

Page 4 - "Category:Square Pianos - Wikimedia Commons." 2014. Wikimedia.Org. 2014. https://commons.wikimedia.org/wiki/Category:Square_pianos.

Saff, Kevin. "Scott Joplin Home." Flickr, www.flickr.com/photos/kevinsaff/190179695/.

Page 5, 10 - "File:Maple Leaf Rag.PNG - Wikimedia Commons." 2014. Wikimedia.Org. 2014. https://commons.wikimedia.org/w/index.php?title=File:Maple_Leaf_Rag.PNG&oldid=143981163.

Wikipedia Contributors. 2020. "List of Compositions by Scott Joplin." Wikipedia. Wikimedia Foundation. January 20, 2020. https://en.wikipedia.org/wiki/List_of_compositions_by_Scott_Joplin#/media/File:Solace_Rag.jpg.

Wikipedia Contributors. 2019. "The Ragtime Dance." Wikipedia. Wikimedia Foundation. December 19, 2019. https://en.wikipedia.org/wiki/The_Ragtime_Dance#/media/File:RagtimeDanceJoplinCover.jpg.

Wikipedia Contributors. 2019a. "The Entertainer (Rag)." Wikipedia. Wikimedia Foundation. December 19, 2019. https://en.wikipedia.org/wiki/The_Entertainer_(rag)#/media/File:EntertainerJoplinCover.JPEG.

Page 6 - Joplin, Scott, and Scott Joplin. "The Chrysanthemum." John Stark, monographic, 1904. Notated Music. https://www.loc.gov/item/ihas.200033248/.

Wikipedia Contributors. 2019. "Bethena." Wikipedia. Wikimedia Foundation. September 27, 2019. https://en.wikipedia.org/wiki/Bethena#/media/File:Bethena.jpg.

Page 7 - "Category:Content Donations by Museum of Science and Technology Belgrade - Wikimedia Commons." 2018. Wikimedia.Org. 2018. https://commons.wikimedia.org/wiki/Category:Content_donations_by_Museum_of_Science_and_Technology_Belgrade.

Wikipedia Contributors. 2020a. "File:Signature of Scott Joplin.Svg." Wikipedia. Wikimedia Foundation. 2020. https://en.wikipedia.org/wiki/File:Signature_of_Scott_Joplin.svg.

Page 17 - Gardner, James. 2013. "Offseason Story Time: The Crash at Crush." Good Bull Hunting. March 5, 2013. http://www.goodbullhunting.com/2013/3/5/4037246/offseason-story-time-the-crash-at-crush.

"File:CrashCrushTx.Jpg - Wikimedia Commons." 2018. Wikimedia.Org. 2018. https://commons.wikimedia.org/wiki/File:CrashCrushTx.jpg.

Page 19 - "Free Sheet Music : Joplin, Scott - The Great Crush Collision March (Piano Solo)." 2020. Free-Scores.Com. 2020. https://www.free-scores.com/download-sheet-music.php?pdf=16964. Excerpt from "The Crush Collision March", Scott Joplin, 1899. Public Domain.

Page 21 - Wikipedia Contributors. 2019. "Crush." Wikipedia. Wikimedia Foundation. December 19, 2019. https://en.wikipedia.org/wiki/Crush.

Page 27 - "[Theodore Roosevelt, Three Quarter Length Portrait, Facing Front]." 2020. Loc.Gov. 2020. https://www.loc.gov/pictures/item/2009631526/.

Page 28 - "[Booker T. Washington, Half-Length Portrait, Seated]." 2020. Loc.Gov. 2020. https://www.loc.gov/pictures/item/2010645746/.

Page 29 - "File:A GUEST OF HONOR Advertising Poster.Jpg - Wikimedia Commons." 1903. Wikimedia.Org. September 2, 1903. https://commons.wikimedia.org/w/index.php?title=File:A_GUEST_OF_HONOR_advertising_poster.jpg&oldid=330964882.

Page 30 - Wikimedia Commons contributors, "File:Tinpanalley.jpg," Wikimedia Commons, the free media repository, https://commons.wikimedia.org/w/index.php?title=File:Tinpanalley.jpg&oldid=211529374 (accessed July 26, 2019).

Page 33 - Wikimedia Commons contributors, "File:Magnetic Rag.jpg," Wikimedia Commons, the free media repository, https://commons.wikimedia.org/w/index.php?title=File:Magnetic_Rag.jpg&oldid=331159244 (accessed July 27, 2019).

Page 34 - *New York Age*. 1917. "Scott Joplin Dies of Mental Trouble," April 5, 1917.

Page 37 - *Treemonisha* poster. United States Public Domain.

Page 38 - Jackson, Curtis. "Scott Joplin (1868-1917) - Find A Grave Memorial." Find A Grave, www.findagrave.com/memorial/556/Scott-Joplin.

Page 39 - Sears, Benjamin. "Scott Joplin (1868-1917) - Find A Grave Memorial." Find A Grave, www.findagrave.com/memorial/556/Scott-Joplin.

Quester, Mark. 2020. "Flickr." Scott Joplin TxHM January 25, 2020. https://www.flickr.com/photos/0ccam/2812379689.

Page 40 - Masinda, Gail. © 2018 Gail Masinda, personal collection, Scott Joplin Park.

Page 41 - Masinda, Gail. © 2018 Gail Masinda, personal collection, First Day Cover.

Walk of Fame - Wikimedia Commons contributors, "File:Scott Joplin St.Louis Walk of Fame 1996.jpg," Wikimedia Commons, the free media repository, https://commons.wikimedia.org/w/index.php?title=File:Scott_Joplin_St.Louis_Walk_of_Fame_1996.jpg&oldid=135415949 (accessed July 15, 2019).

Page 42 - Walters, Robert. n.d. Scott Joplin International Ragtime Foundation.

Mallette, David. n.d. Regional Music Heritage Center.

Page 43, 44 - Masinda, Gail © 2018 Gail Masinda, personal collection.

Page 45 - Masinda, Gail © 2018 Gail Masinda, personal collection, Scott Joplin mural, 311 Main Street, Texarkana, AR.

Recommended Recordings
The Complete Piano Works of Scott Joplin, recorded by Richard Dowling
http://www.richard-dowling.com/recordings.html

Wow! That was quite a story. Scott Joplin was truly a remarkable man!

What was your favorite part of the story?

A printable companion book filled with activities about Scott Joplin is available in the Maestro Heights Store. You will find some free printables in the Store, too.

"Our history is full of stories about remarkable people. Visit the Maestro Heights Museum to see more exhibits."

"'Bye for now!"

www.ingramcontent.com/pod-product-compliance
Lightning Source LLC
Chambersburg PA
CBHW042247100526
44587CB00002B/57